Formulae
for
advanced
with
statistical tables

SECOND EDITION

Cambridge University Press

Cambridge

New York   Port Chester

Melbourne   Sydney

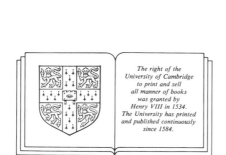

CONTENTS

Published by the Press Syndicate of the University of Cambridge
The Pitt Building, Trumpington Street, Cambridge CB2 1RP
40 West 20th Street, New York, NY 10011–4211, USA
10 Stamford Road, Oakleigh, Melbourne 3166, Australia

First published 1984
Second edition 1989
Third printing 1991

Printed in Great Britain
by GreenShires Print Ltd, Kettering

ISBN 0 521 36773 5
(ISBN 0 521 31920 X first edition)
TS

Series

$\sum_{i=1}^{n} i = \frac{1}{2}n(n+1)$ (an **arithmetic progression**); $\sum_{i=1}^{n} i^2 = \frac{1}{6}n(n+1)(2n+1)$; $\sum_{i=1}^{n} i^3 = \frac{1}{4}n^2(n+1)^2$.

$$\sum_{i=1}^{n} i(i+1)(i+2)\ldots(i+r) = \frac{1}{r+2}\, n(n+1)(n+2)\ldots(n+r+1).$$

$\sum_{i=1}^{n} x^{i-1} = \dfrac{1-x^n}{1-x}$ [use if $x<1$] or $\dfrac{x^n-1}{x-1}$ [use if $x>1$] (**a geometric progression**);

if $|x|<1$, $\sum_{i=1}^{\infty} x^{i-1} = \dfrac{1}{1-x}$.

Logarithms, exponentials and hyperbolic functions

$y = b^x \Leftrightarrow x = \log_b y$; $y = e^x$ (or $\exp x$) $\Leftrightarrow x = \ln y$ (or $\log_e y$).

$q^x = \exp(x \ln q)$.

$\log_b x = \log_c x / \log_c b$; in particular, $\log_b x = \ln x / \ln b$.

To any base, $\log 1 = 0$; $\log(xy) = \log x + \log y$; $\log(x/y) = \log x - \log y$; $\log x^k = k \log x$.

$\sinh x = \frac{1}{2}(e^x - e^{-x})$; $\cosh x = \frac{1}{2}(e^x + e^{-x})$; $\tanh x = \sinh x / \cosh x$.

$\sinh^{-1} x = \ln\{x + \sqrt{(1+x^2)}\}$; $\cosh^{-1} x = \ln\{x + \sqrt{(x^2-1)}\}$ [$x \geqslant 1$];

$\tanh^{-1} x = \frac{1}{2}\ln\{(1+x)/(1-x)\}$ [$-1 < x < 1$].

Factorials

$0! = 1, \quad (i+1)! = (i+1) \times i! \quad \text{for } i = 0, 1, 2, \ldots$

For large values of n, **Stirling's approximation** is $\ln(n!) \approx \frac{1}{2}\ln(2\pi) + (n+\frac{1}{2})\ln n - n + \dfrac{1}{12n}$.

Binomial coefficients (*i* denotes a natural number.)

For any real n, $\dbinom{n}{i} = \dfrac{n(n-1)\ldots(n-i+1)}{i!}$.

This may be calculated from the inductive definition $\dbinom{n}{0} = 1, \quad \dbinom{n}{i+1} = \dfrac{n-i}{i+1}\dbinom{n}{i} \quad \text{for } i = 0, 1, 2, \ldots$

The 'Pascal triangle' rule: $\dbinom{n+1}{i} = \dbinom{n}{i-1} + \dbinom{n}{i}$.

If n is also a natural number, and if ${}_nC_i$ denotes the number of subsets of i elements contained in a set of n elements, then

$$ {}_nC_i = \binom{n}{i} = \frac{n!}{i!(n-i)!}. $$

The binomial theorem: If n is a natural number, $(b+a)^n = \sum_{i=0}^{n} \dbinom{n}{i} b^{n-i} a^i$.

(See also p. 17 for the generalised binomial series for $(1+x)^m$, p. 37 for binomial probability and p. 38 for a table of binomial coefficients.)

Completing the square: If $a \neq 0$, $\quad ax^2 + bx + c = a\left(x + \dfrac{b}{2a}\right)^2 + \dfrac{4ac - b^2}{4a}$,

so that

$$ax^2 + bx + c = 0 \Leftrightarrow x = \frac{-b \pm \sqrt{(b^2 - 4ac)}}{2a}.$$

If the roots are denoted by α, β, then $\quad \alpha + \beta = -b/a, \quad \alpha\beta = c/a.$

In real algebra, if $a \neq 0$, $ax^2 + bx + c > 0$ for all $x \Leftrightarrow a > 0$ and $4ac - b^2 > 0$.

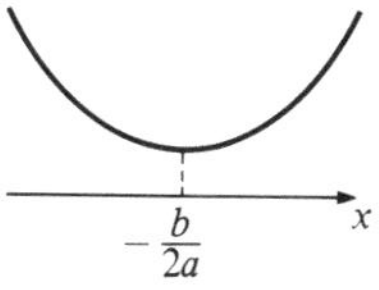

$a > 0,\ 4ac - b^2 > 0$

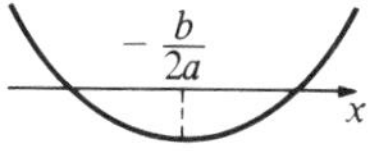

$a > 0,\ 4ac - b^2 < 0$

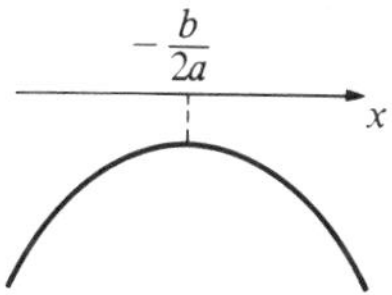

$a < 0,\ 4ac - b^2 > 0$

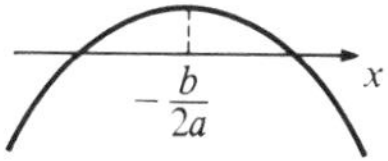

$a < 0,\ 4ac - b^2 < 0$

Cubic equations

If $a \neq 0$ and the roots of $ax^3 + bx^2 + cx + d = 0$ are α, β, γ, then

$$\alpha + \beta + \gamma = -b/a, \quad \beta\gamma + \gamma\alpha + \alpha\beta = c/a, \quad \alpha\beta\gamma = -d/a.$$

Complex numbers

$z = a + bj$ (a, b real) has **real part** $\operatorname{Re} z = a$ and **imaginary part** $\operatorname{Im} z = b$, with $j^2 = -1$.

The **modulus** $|z|$ and **argument** $\arg z$ are defined by:

$|z| = \sqrt{(a^2 + b^2)}$; $\arg z$ is a number (in radians) whose sine is $b/|z|$ and whose cosine is $a/|z|$ $[z \neq 0]$.

(Two conventions are in use for the principal value of $\arg z$: either $0 \leqslant \arg z < 2\pi$ or $-\pi < \arg z \leqslant \pi$.)

The **modulus–argument form** of z is $z = [r, \theta] = r(\cos\theta + j\sin\theta) = r\exp(\theta j)$, where r, θ are real.

The product rule: $[r, \theta] \times [s, \phi] = [rs, \theta + \phi]$.

De Moivre's theorem for integral index: $[1, \theta]^n = [1, n\theta]$, or $(\cos\theta + j\sin\theta)^n = \cos n\theta + j\sin n\theta$.
The roots of $z^n = 1$ are $z = [1, 2\pi k/n] = \exp\{2\pi(k/n)j\}$ for $k = 0, 1, 2, \ldots, n-1$. In particular, the roots of $z^3 = 1$ are $1, \omega, \omega^2$, where $\omega = \cos\frac{2}{3}\pi + j\sin\frac{2}{3}\pi = -\frac{1}{2} + (\frac{1}{2}\sqrt{3})j$, so that $\omega^3 = 1$ and $1 + \omega + \omega^2 = 0$.

The **conjugate** complex number z^* (also written $\bar{z}$) is $z^* = a - bj$, so that

$$z + z^* = 2\operatorname{Re} z, \quad zz^* = |z|^2 \quad \text{and} \quad \frac{1}{z} = \frac{z^*}{|z|^2} = \frac{a}{a^2+b^2} - \frac{b}{a^2+b^2}j;$$

$$(z_1 + z_2)^* = z_1^* + z_2^*, \quad (z_1 z_2)^* = z_1^* z_2^*.$$

(The letter i is often used instead of j in writing complex numbers.)

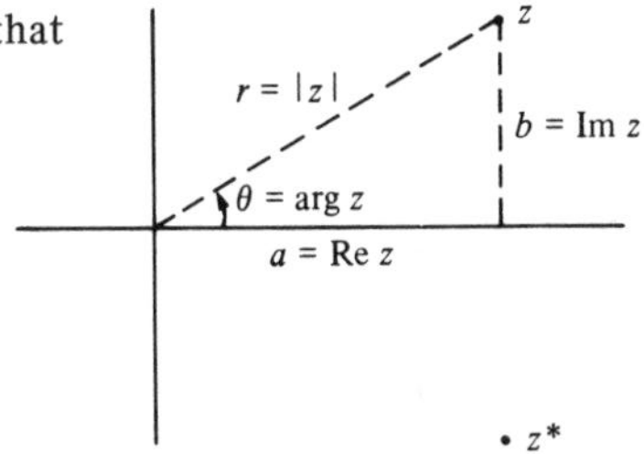

Matrices (Transformations $\mathbf{v} \mapsto \mathbf{Mv}$, where $\mathbf{v}$ is the appropriate column matrix.)

Rotation through θ about O: $\mathbf{M} = \begin{bmatrix} \cos\theta & -\sin\theta \\ \sin\theta & \cos\theta \end{bmatrix}$. Reflection in $y = x\tan\theta$: $\mathbf{M} = \begin{bmatrix} \cos 2\theta & \sin 2\theta \\ \sin 2\theta & -\cos 2\theta \end{bmatrix}$.

Determinants: If $\mathbf{M} = \begin{bmatrix} a_1 & b_1 \\ a_2 & b_2 \end{bmatrix}$, $\det \mathbf{M} = a_1 b_2 - a_2 b_1$.

Its magnitude measures the area scale factor of the transformation.

If $\mathbf{M} = \begin{bmatrix} a_1 & b_1 & c_1 \\ a_2 & b_2 & c_2 \\ a_3 & b_3 & c_3 \end{bmatrix}$, $\det \mathbf{M} = a_1(b_2 c_3 - b_3 c_2) - a_2(b_1 c_3 - b_3 c_1) + a_3(b_1 c_2 - b_2 c_1)$.

Its magnitude measures the volume scale factor of the transformation.

An **eigenvector** of $\mathbf{M}$ is a non-zero vector $\mathbf{x}$ such that $\mathbf{Mx} = \lambda\mathbf{x}$; λ is the corresponding **eigenvalue**. The eigenvalues satisfy the **characteristic equation** $\det(\mathbf{M} - \lambda\mathbf{I}) = 0$. If $\mathbf{M}$ has a full set of independent eigenvectors, then $\mathbf{M} = \mathbf{U}\Lambda\mathbf{U}^{-1}$, where $\mathbf{U}$ is the matrix of eigenvectors and Λ is the diagonal matrix of eigenvalues.

An **orthogonal** matrix satisfies $\mathbf{M}^{\mathrm{T}}\mathbf{M} = \mathbf{I}$, where $\mathbf{M}^{\mathrm{T}}$ is the transpose of $\mathbf{M}$; that is, $\mathbf{M}^{\mathrm{T}} = \mathbf{M}^{-1}$.

A **symmetric matrix** has the property that $\mathbf{M}^{\mathrm{T}} = \mathbf{M}$. A symmetric matrix with real elements has real eigenvalues and a full set of real independent eigenvectors. The matrix of eigenvectors, $\mathbf{U}$, can be chosen to be orthogonal, so that $\mathbf{M} = \mathbf{U}\Lambda\mathbf{U}^{\mathrm{T}}$; that is, $\mathbf{U}^{\mathrm{T}}\mathbf{MU}$ is the diagonal matrix of eigenvalues.

ALGEBRAIC STRUCTURE

Binary operations on a set

Denoting the set by S and the operation by $*$:

The set is **closed** with respect to the operation if, for all $a, b \in S$, $\quad a * b \in S$.
An **identity** (or **neutral**) **element** is an element $i \in S$ such that, for all $a \in S$, $\quad i * a = a * i = a$.
The **inverse** of an element $a \in S$ is an element $a^{-1} \in S$ such that $\quad a * a^{-1} = a^{-1} * a = i$.
The operation is **associative** if, for all $a, b, c \in S$, $\quad (a * b) * c = a * (b * c)$
The operation is **commutative** if, for all $a, b \in S$, $\quad a * b = b * a$.

For two operations $*$, $\circ$:

The operation $*$ is **distributive** over the operation $\circ$ if, for all $a, b, c \in S$,

$$a * (b \circ c) = (a * b) \circ (a * c) \quad \text{and} \quad (b \circ c) * a = (b * a) \circ (c * a).$$

Particular structures

Group $(G, *)$

Single binary operation $*$
G is closed under $*$
$*$ is associative
An identity element exists
Every element has an inverse

Ring $(S, +, .)$

Under operation $+$
Abelian group (identity written as 0, inverse of a as $-a$)

Under operation $.$
S is closed
Associative

$.$ is distributive over $+$

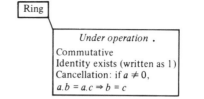

Group

$*$ is commutative

Ring

Under operation .

Commutative
Identity exists (written as 1)
Cancellation: if $a \neq 0$,
$a.b = a.c \Rightarrow b = c$

Field $(F, +, .)$

Under operation +

Abelian group (identity written as 0, inverse of a as $-a$)

Under operation .

Elements excluding 0 form an Abelian group (identity written as 1, inverse of a as a^{-1})

. is distributive over +

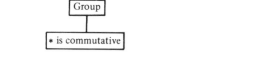

Vector (or linear) space $V = \{\mathbf{a}, \mathbf{b}, \mathbf{c}, \ldots\}$ over a field $F = (\{\lambda, \mu, \nu, \ldots\}, +, .)$

Abelian group $(V, +)$
(see note)

For all $\lambda, \mu \in F$ and all $\mathbf{a}, \mathbf{b} \in V$:

$\lambda\mathbf{a} \in V$
$\lambda(\mathbf{a} + \mathbf{b}) = \lambda\mathbf{a} + \lambda\mathbf{b}$
$(\lambda + \mu)\mathbf{a} = \lambda\mathbf{a} + \mu\mathbf{a}$
$(\lambda.\mu)\mathbf{a} = \lambda(\mu\mathbf{a})$
$1\mathbf{a} = \mathbf{a}$

Note: Strictly, this binary operation + is not the same + as in the field F, since it operates on a different set of elements. It is, however, customary to use the same symbol for the two. The elements of V are called **vectors**, and the elements of F **scalars.**

Relations between elements of a set

Denoting the set by S and the relation by R:

The relation is **reflexive** if, for all $a \in S$, $\quad aRa$.
The relation is **symmetric** if, for all $a, b \in S$, $\quad aRb \Rightarrow bRa$.
The relation is **transitive** if, for all $a, b, c \in S$, $\quad (aRb \text{ and } bRc) \Rightarrow aRc$.

An **equivalence relation** is a relation which is reflexive, symmetric and transitive.

Relations between structures

An **isomorphism** between two groups $(G, *)$ and $(H, \circ)$ is a one–one mapping such that, if $a \leftrightarrow x$ and $b \leftrightarrow y$ (where $a, b \in G, x, y \in H$), then $\quad a * b \leftrightarrow x \circ y$.

A **homomorphism** between two groups $(G, *)$ and $(H, \circ)$ is a mapping such that, if $a \rightarrow x$ and $b \rightarrow y$, then $a * b \rightarrow x \circ y$.

Isomorphisms and homomorphisms between other pairs of structures are defined similarly.

Number sets

Type of number	Symbol	Description	Structure
Natural	$\mathbb{N}$	$\{1, 2, 3, \ldots\}$ (or sometimes $\{0, 1, 2, 3, \ldots\}$)	–
Integer	$\mathbb{Z}$	$\{0, \pm 1, \pm 2, \pm 3, \ldots\}$	Integral domain
Rational	$\mathbb{Q}$	$\{p/q : p \in \mathbb{Z}, q \in \mathbb{Z}^+\}$	Field
Real	$\mathbb{R}$	–	Field
Complex	$\mathbb{C}$	$\{a + bj : a, b \in \mathbb{R}\}$	Field
Integer mod n	$\mathbb{Z}_n$	$\{0, 1, 2, \ldots, n-1\}$ under $+, \cdot$ mod n, $n \in \mathbb{N}, n \geqslant 2$	Ring (field if n is prime)

Products

If $\mathbf{a}$, $\mathbf{b}$ are two vectors in three-dimensional space with magnitudes a, b, and if the angle between them is θ (where $0 \leqslant \theta \leqslant \pi$), then

$\mathbf{a}\,.\,\mathbf{b}$ is a scalar of magnitude $ab\cos\theta$;

$\mathbf{a} \times \mathbf{b}$ is a vector of magnitude $ab\sin\theta$, in a direction perpendicular to both $\mathbf{a}$ and $\mathbf{b}$ such that $\mathbf{a}$, $\mathbf{b}$, $\mathbf{a} \times \mathbf{b}$ form a right-handed triple.

If the vectors $\mathbf{a}$, $\mathbf{b}$ are represented by column matrices $\begin{bmatrix} a_1 \\ a_2 \\ a_3 \end{bmatrix}$, $\begin{bmatrix} b_1 \\ b_2 \\ b_3 \end{bmatrix}$ of their components with respect to a rectangular system of right-handed axes, or as $a_1\mathbf{i} + a_2\mathbf{j} + a_3\mathbf{k}$, $b_1\mathbf{i} + b_2\mathbf{j} + b_3\mathbf{k}$, then

$$\mathbf{a}\,.\,\mathbf{b} = a_1 b_1 + a_2 b_2 + a_3 b_3;$$

$$\mathbf{a} \times \mathbf{b} = \begin{bmatrix} a_2 b_3 - a_3 b_2 \\ a_3 b_1 - a_1 b_3 \\ a_1 b_2 - a_2 b_1 \end{bmatrix} = (a_2 b_3 - a_3 b_2)\mathbf{i} + (a_3 b_1 - a_1 b_3)\mathbf{j} + (a_1 b_2 - a_2 b_1)\mathbf{k}.$$

Scalar triple product: $[\mathbf{a}\ \mathbf{b}\ \mathbf{c}] = \mathbf{a}\,.\,(\mathbf{b} \times \mathbf{c}) = \mathbf{b}\,.\,(\mathbf{c} \times \mathbf{a}) = \mathbf{c}\,.\,(\mathbf{a} \times \mathbf{b}) = \det \begin{bmatrix} a_1 & b_1 & c_1 \\ a_2 & b_2 & c_2 \\ a_3 & b_3 & c_3 \end{bmatrix}$.

Vector triple product: $\mathbf{a} \times (\mathbf{b} \times \mathbf{c}) = (\mathbf{a}\,.\,\mathbf{c})\mathbf{b} - (\mathbf{a}\,.\,\mathbf{b})\mathbf{c}$; $\quad (\mathbf{a} \times \mathbf{b}) \times \mathbf{c} = (\mathbf{a}\,.\,\mathbf{c})\mathbf{b} - (\mathbf{b}\,.\,\mathbf{c})\mathbf{a}$.

Area of a parallelogram with edges $\mathbf{a}$, $\mathbf{b}$ is $|\mathbf{a} \times \mathbf{b}|$.

Volume of a parallelepiped with edges $\mathbf{a}$, $\mathbf{b}$, $\mathbf{c}$ is $|[\mathbf{a}\ \mathbf{b}\ \mathbf{c}]|$.

Linear dependence

Vectors **u**, **v**, **w** are linearly dependent if scalars λ, μ, ν (not all zero) exist such that $\lambda\mathbf{u} + \mu\mathbf{v} + \nu\mathbf{w} = \mathbf{0}$ (and similarly for more or fewer than three vectors).

Lines and planes

(**a**, **b**, **c**, **r** stand for position vectors of points A, B, C, R relative to an origin O. The results apply only in non-degenerate situations: two points A, B are not coincident, three points A, B, C are not collinear.)

R lies on the line $AB \Leftrightarrow \mathbf{r} = \lambda\mathbf{a} + \mu\mathbf{b}$ with $\lambda + \mu = 1$.

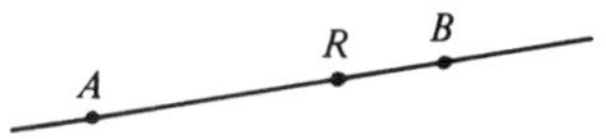

R lies on the plane $ABC \Leftrightarrow \mathbf{r} = \lambda\mathbf{a} + \mu\mathbf{b} + \nu\mathbf{c}$ with $\lambda + \mu + \nu = 1$.

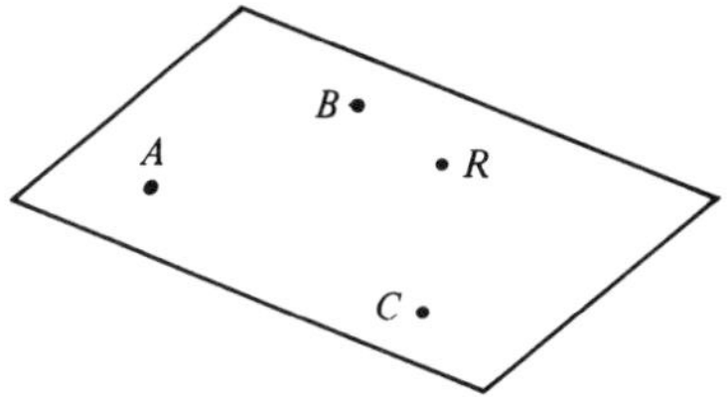

In the **two-dimensional case**, if $\lambda \neq 0$, R is the point of the line such that $AR/RB = \mu/\lambda$. Thus if R divides AB in the ratio $p:q$, then

$$\mathbf{r} = \frac{q}{p+q}\,\mathbf{a} + \frac{p}{p+q}\,\mathbf{b}.$$

Gradient (two dimensions only): The vector $\begin{bmatrix} a \\ b \end{bmatrix}$, where $a \neq 0$, has gradient $m = b/a$. The equation of the line through (x_1, y_1) with gradient m is $y - y_1 = m(x - x_1)$.

Parametric equations: The equation $\mathbf{r} = \mathbf{a} + \lambda\mathbf{d}$ represents a line through A with direction vector $\mathbf{d}$.

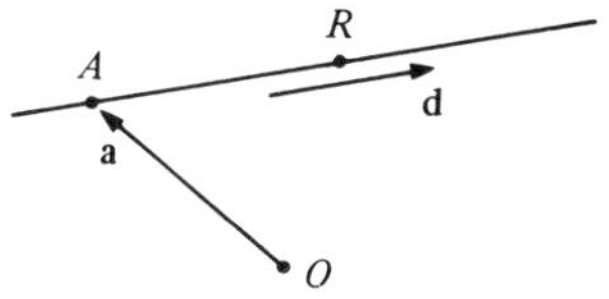

In component form, $\begin{bmatrix} x \\ y \\ z \end{bmatrix} = \begin{bmatrix} a_1 \\ a_2 \\ a_3 \end{bmatrix} + \lambda \begin{bmatrix} d_1 \\ d_2 \\ d_3 \end{bmatrix}$.

In cartesian form, $\dfrac{x - a_1}{d_1} = \dfrac{y - a_2}{d_2} = \dfrac{z - a_3}{d_3}$.

The equation $\mathbf{r} = \mathbf{a} + \lambda\mathbf{d} + \mu\mathbf{e}$, where $\mathbf{d}$ and $\mathbf{e}$ are independent, represents a plane through A parallel to the vectors $\mathbf{d}$ and $\mathbf{e}$.

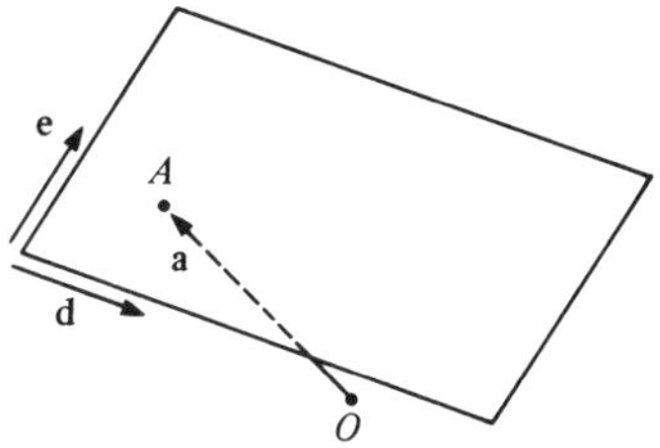

Normal equations: The vector $\mathbf{n} = \begin{bmatrix} a \\ b \\ c \end{bmatrix}$ is perpendicular to the plane $ax + by + cz = d$, or $\mathbf{n} \cdot \mathbf{r} = d$.

The distance from any point R_1 to this plane is $|\mathbf{n} \cdot \mathbf{r}_1 - d|/n$, where n is the magnitude of the normal vector $\mathbf{n}$. In cartesian form, the distance from (x_1, y_1, z_1) to the plane is

$$\frac{|ax_1 + by_1 + cz_1 - d|}{\sqrt{(a^2 + b^2 + c^2)}}.$$

Similar results apply in two dimensions; e.g. $\mathbf{n} = \begin{bmatrix} a \\ b \end{bmatrix}$ is perpendicular to the line $ax + by = d$.

TRIGONOMETRY

$$\sec\theta = \frac{1}{\cos\theta}, \quad \tan\theta = \frac{\sin\theta}{\cos\theta} \quad [\theta \neq (k+\tfrac{1}{2})\pi];$$

$$\operatorname{cosec}\theta \text{ (or } \csc\theta) = \frac{1}{\sin\theta}, \quad \cot\theta = \frac{1}{\tan\theta} = \frac{\cos\theta}{\sin\theta} \quad [\theta \neq k\pi].$$

Pythagoras formulae: $\cos^2\theta + \sin^2\theta = 1;\qquad 1+\tan^2\theta = \sec^2\theta;\qquad \cot^2\theta + 1 = \operatorname{cosec}^2\theta.$

Addition formulae: $\sin(\theta \pm \phi) = \sin\theta\cos\phi \pm \cos\theta\sin\phi;\qquad \cos(\theta \pm \phi) = \cos\theta\cos\phi \mp \sin\theta\sin\phi;$

$$\tan(\theta \pm \phi) = \frac{\tan\theta \pm \tan\phi}{1 \mp \tan\theta\tan\phi}.$$

Double angle formulae: $\sin 2\theta = 2\sin\theta\cos\theta;\qquad \cos 2\theta = \cos^2\theta - \sin^2\theta;\qquad \tan 2\theta = \dfrac{2\tan\theta}{1-\tan^2\theta}.$

$$2\cos^2\theta = 1 + \cos 2\theta; \qquad 2\sin^2\theta = 1 - \cos 2\theta.$$

If $t = \tan\frac{1}{2}\theta$, then

$$\sin\theta = \frac{2t}{1+t^2}; \qquad \cos\theta = \frac{1-t^2}{1+t^2}; \qquad \tan\theta = \frac{2t}{1-t^2}; \qquad \frac{d\theta}{dt} = \frac{2}{1+t^2}.$$

Sum and difference formulae: $2\cos\theta\cos\phi = \cos(\theta+\phi) + \cos(\theta-\phi);$

$$2\sin\theta\sin\phi = \cos(\theta-\phi) - \cos(\theta+\phi);$$

$$2\sin\theta\cos\phi = \sin(\theta+\phi) + \sin(\theta-\phi)$$

$$\sin\alpha - \sin\beta = 2\cos\tfrac{1}{2}(\alpha+\beta)\sin\tfrac{1}{2}(\alpha-\beta);$$

$$\cos\alpha + \cos\beta = 2\cos\tfrac{1}{2}(\alpha+\beta)\cos\tfrac{1}{2}(\alpha-\beta);$$

$$\cos\alpha - \cos\beta = 2\sin\tfrac{1}{2}(\alpha+\beta)\sin\tfrac{1}{2}(\beta-\alpha).$$

Symmetry and periodicity:

	$-\theta$	$\frac{1}{2}\pi-\theta$	$\frac{1}{2}\pi+\theta$	$\pi-\theta$	$\pi+\theta$	$2\pi-\theta$	$2\pi+\theta$
sin	$-\sin\theta$	$\cos\theta$	$\cos\theta$	$\sin\theta$	$-\sin\theta$	$-\sin\theta$	$\sin\theta$
cos	$\cos\theta$	$\sin\theta$	$-\sin\theta$	$-\cos\theta$	$-\cos\theta$	$\cos\theta$	$\cos\theta$

Ranges of the inverse functions: $-\frac{1}{2}\pi \leqslant \sin^{-1}x \leqslant \frac{1}{2}\pi$, $\quad 0 \leqslant \cos^{-1}x \leqslant \pi \quad [-1 \leqslant x \leqslant 1]$;

$-\frac{1}{2}\pi < \tan^{-1}x < \frac{1}{2}\pi$.

(The notation $\arcsin x$, $\arccos x$, $\arctan x$ is also used.)

Triangle formulae: In the triangle ABC,

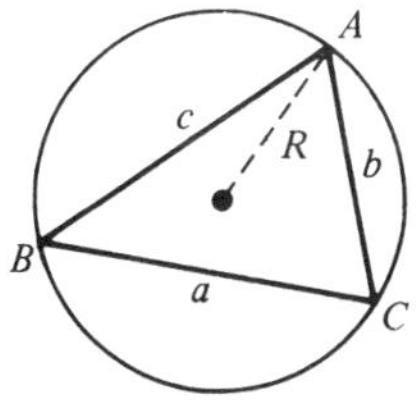

$$\frac{a}{\sin A} = \frac{b}{\sin B} = \frac{c}{\sin C} = 2R \quad \text{(the **sine rule**)};$$

$$a^2 = b^2 + c^2 - 2bc\cos A, \quad \text{or} \quad \cos A = \frac{b^2+c^2-a^2}{2bc}, \text{ etc.} \quad \text{(the **cosine rule**)};$$

$$\text{area} = \tfrac{1}{2}bc\sin A, \text{ etc.}$$

$$= \sqrt{\{s(s-a)(s-b)(s-c)\}}, \quad \text{where } s = \tfrac{1}{2}(a+b+c).$$

CALCULUS

If $\dfrac{f(x) - f(a)}{x - a}$ tends to a limit as x tends to a, then f is said to be **differentiable** at a. The limit is called the **derivative** of f at a and is usually written $f'(a)$. The function f' is called the **derived function** of f.

f(x)	f′(x)	f(x)	f′(x)	f(x)	f′(x)	f(x)	f′(x)
x^n	nx^{n-1}	$\sin x$	$\cos x$	$\tan x$	$\sec^2 x$	$\sinh x$	$\cosh x$
$e^x (= \exp x)$	$e^x (= \exp x)$	$\cos x$	$-\sin x$	$\sec x$	$\sec x \tan x$	$\cosh x$	$\sinh x$
q^x	$q^x \ln q$	$\sin^{-1} x$	$1/\sqrt{(1 - x^2)}$	$\cot x$	$-\mathrm{cosec}^2 x$	$\sinh^{-1} x$	$1/\sqrt{(1 + x^2)}$
$\ln x\ (= \log_e x)$	$1/x$	$\tan^{-1} x$	$1/(1 + x^2)$	$\mathrm{cosec}\, x$	$-\mathrm{cosec}\, x \cot x$	$\cosh^{-1} x$	$1/\sqrt{(x^2 - 1)}$

Product rule: If $y = uv$, then $\dfrac{dy}{dx} = \dfrac{du}{dx} v + u \dfrac{dv}{dx}$.

Quotient rule: If $y = \dfrac{u}{v}$, then $\dfrac{dy}{dx} = \left(\dfrac{du}{dx} v - u \dfrac{dv}{dx}\right) \Big/ v^2$.

Chain rule: If $y = f(u)$ and $u = g(x)$, then $\dfrac{dy}{dx} = \dfrac{dy}{du} \times \dfrac{du}{dx}$.

Taylor's polynomial approximation

For small h $\quad f(a + h) \approx f(a) + f'(a) \,.\, h + \dfrac{1}{2!} f''(a) \,.\, h^2 + \ldots + \dfrac{1}{n!} f^{(n)}(a) \,.\, h^n$.

The remainder (error) can be expressed as $\dfrac{1}{(n + 1)!} f^{(n+1)}(\xi) . h^{n+1}$, where ξ is some number

between a and $a + h$

Applications to particular functions

$$(1+h)^m \approx 1 + mh + \frac{m(m-1)}{2!}h^2 + \ldots + \binom{m}{n}h^n.$$

$$\ln(1+h) \approx h - \frac{h^2}{2} + \frac{h^3}{3} - \ldots + (-1)^{n+1}\frac{h^n}{n}.$$

$$e^h \approx 1 + h + \frac{h^2}{2!} + \ldots + \frac{h^n}{n!}.$$

$$\cosh h \approx 1 + \frac{h^2}{2!} + \frac{h^4}{4!} + \ldots + \frac{h^{2k}}{(2k)!}.$$

$$\sinh h \approx h + \frac{h^3}{3!} + \ldots + \frac{h^{2k+1}}{(2k+1)!}.$$

$$\cos h \approx 1 - \frac{h^2}{2!} + \frac{h^4}{4!} + \ldots + (-1)^k\frac{h^{2k}}{(2k)!}.$$

$$\sin h \approx h - \frac{h^3}{3!} + \ldots + (-1)^k\frac{h^{2k+1}}{(2k+1)!}.$$

$$\tan^{-1} h \approx h - \frac{h^3}{3} + \frac{h^5}{5} - \ldots + (-1)^k\frac{h^{2k+1}}{2k+1}.$$

Power series with intervals of validity

$$(1+x)^m = \sum_{i=0}^{\infty}\binom{m}{i}x^i$$ for $|x| < 1$ and sometimes also for $x = 1$ and/or $x = -1$.

$$\ln(1+x) = \sum_{i=1}^{\infty}(-1)^{i+1}\frac{x^i}{i} \quad \text{for } -1 < x \leqslant 1.$$

$$e^x = \sum_{i=0}^{\infty}\frac{x^i}{i!} \quad \text{for all } x.$$

$$\cosh x = \sum_{i=0}^{\infty}\frac{x^{2i}}{(2i)!} \quad \text{for all } x.$$

$$\sinh x = \sum_{i=0}^{\infty}\frac{x^{2i+1}}{(2i+1)!} \quad \text{for all } x.$$

$$\cos x = \sum_{i=0}^{\infty}(-1)^i\frac{x^{2i}}{(2i)!} \quad \text{for all } x.$$

$$\sin x = \sum_{i=0}^{\infty}(-1)^i\frac{x^{2i+1}}{(2i+1)!} \quad \text{for all } x.$$

$$\tan^{-1} x = \sum_{i=0}^{\infty}(-1)^i\frac{x^{2i+1}}{2i+1} \quad \text{for } |x| \leqslant 1.$$

Indefinite integrals (In the following we take $a > 0$ and omit the additive constant.)

f(x)	$\int$ f(x) dx	f(x)	$\int$ f(x) dx
$x^n \quad (n \neq -1)$	$x^{n+1}/(n+1)$	$\sin x$	$-\cos x$
$1/x$	$\ln \lvert x \rvert, x \neq 0$	$\cos x$	$\sin x$
$\frac{1}{x^2+a^2}$	$\frac{1}{a}\tan^{-1}\frac{x}{a}$	$\tan x$	$\ln \lvert \sec x \rvert$
		$\cot x$	$\ln \lvert \sin x \rvert$
$\frac{1}{x^2-a^2}$	$\frac{1}{2a}\ln\left\lvert\frac{x-a}{x+a}\right\rvert$	$\sec x$	$\ln \lvert \sec x + \tan x \rvert = \ln \lvert \tan(\frac{1}{2}x + \frac{1}{4}\pi) \rvert$
		$\operatorname{cosec} x$	$\ln \lvert \operatorname{cosec} x - \cot x \rvert = \ln \lvert \tan \frac{1}{2}x \rvert$
$\frac{1}{\sqrt{(x^2+a^2)}}$	$\sinh^{-1}\frac{x}{a}$ or	$e^{ax}\sin bx$	$\frac{e^{ax}}{a^2+b^2}(a \sin bx - b \cos bx)$
	$\ln\{x + \sqrt{(a^2+x^2)}\}$	$e^{ax}\cos bx$	$\frac{e^{ax}}{a^2+b^2}(a \cos bx + b \sin bx)$
$\frac{1}{\sqrt{(x^2-a^2)}}$	$\cosh^{-1}\frac{x}{a}$ or	$\sin^2 x$	$\frac{1}{2}(x - \frac{1}{2}\sin 2x)$
	$\ln\{x + \sqrt{(x^2-a^2)}\}$	$\cos^2 x$	$\frac{1}{2}(x + \frac{1}{2}\sin 2x)$
	if $x7a$	$\sinh x$	$\cosh x$
$\frac{1}{\sqrt{(a^2-x^2)}}$	$\sin^{-1}\frac{x}{a}$	$\cosh x$	$\sinh x$

Integration by parts: $\int u \frac{dv}{dx}\,dx = uv - \int \frac{du}{dx} v\,dx.$

Reduction formulae for trigonometric integrals

$$\int_0^{\pi/2} \sin^m x\,dx = \frac{m-1}{m}\int_0^{\pi/2} \sin^{m-2} x\,dx; \qquad \int_0^{\pi/2} \cos^m x\,dx = \frac{m-1}{m}\int_0^{\pi/2} \cos^{m-2} x\,dx;$$

$$\int_0^{\pi/2} \sin^m x \cos^n x\,dx = \frac{m-1}{m+n}\int_0^{\pi/2} \sin^{m-2} x \cos^n x\,dx = \frac{n-1}{m+n}\int_0^{\pi/2} \sin^m x \cos^{n-2} x\,dx.$$

(These results hold provided that the exponents in the reduced form are greater than -1. There are analogous reduction formulae with other intervals of integration $(\frac{1}{2}k_1\pi, \frac{1}{2}k_2\pi)$ with k_1, k_2 integral.)

Multi-dimensional calculus

If a function maps $(x, y) \mapsto (u, v)$, the local linear mapping is described by the **Jacobian matrix**

$$\frac{\partial(u, v)}{\partial(x, y)} = \begin{bmatrix} \partial u/\partial x & \partial u/\partial y \\ \partial v/\partial x & \partial v/\partial y \end{bmatrix}.$$

The method of substitution transforms the multiple integral $\iint f(x, y)\,dx\,dy$ into

$$\iint g(r, s) \left| \det \frac{\partial(x, y)}{\partial(r, s)} \right| dr\,ds,$$ evaluated over the corresponding region.

For polar coordinates $x = r\cos\theta$, $y = r\sin\theta$, $\det \dfrac{\partial(x, y)}{\partial(r, \theta)} = r.$

For spherical polar coordinates $x = r\sin\theta\cos\phi$, $y = r\sin\theta\sin\phi$, $z = r\cos\theta$,

$$\det \frac{\partial(x, y, z)}{\partial(r, \theta, \phi)} = r^2 \sin\theta.$$

Differential geometry

(Primes denote differentiation with respect to a parameter.)

Arc length (s): $(s')^2 = (x')^2 + (y')^2$; $(s')^2 = (r')^2 + (r\theta')^2$.

Tangential direction: $\cos\psi = dx/ds$, $\sin\psi = dy/ds$;

$\cos\phi = dr/ds$, $\sin\phi = r\,d\theta/ds$.

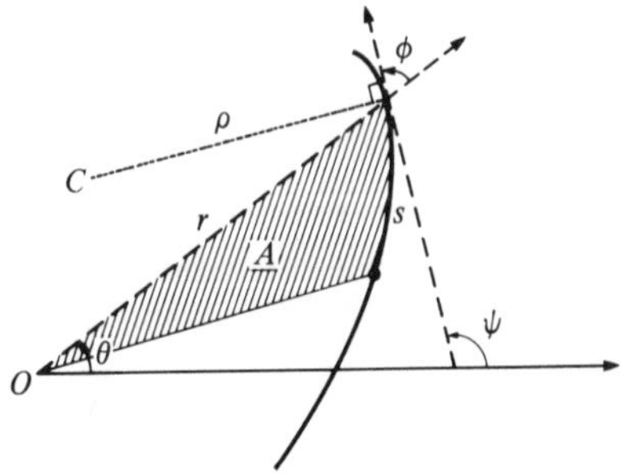

Curvature: $\kappa = \dfrac{d\psi}{ds} = \dfrac{x'y'' - x''y'}{\{(x')^2 + (y')^2\}^{3/2}}$.

Radius of curvature: $\rho = 1/\kappa$.

Area (A): $A' = \frac{1}{2}r^2\theta'$, so that $A = \int \frac{1}{2}r^2 d\theta$ evaluated between appropriate limits.

The perpendicular from O to the tangent is $p = r\sin\phi$.

DIFFERENTIAL AND DIFFERENCE EQUATIONS

First-order linear differential equations

The integrating factor for $\dfrac{dy}{dx} + \mathrm{p}(x)y = \mathrm{q}(x)$ is $\mathrm{r}(x) = \exp\left\{\int_c^x \mathrm{p}(t)\,dt\right\}$; it reduces the equation to

$$\frac{d}{dx}\{\mathrm{r}(x)y\} = \mathrm{r}(x)\mathrm{q}(x).$$

Second-order linear equations

The **auxiliary equation** for

$$\frac{d^2y}{dx^2} + a\frac{dy}{dx} + by = 0, \qquad (1\alpha) \qquad\Bigg|\qquad u_{n+2} + au_{n+1} + bu_n = 0, \qquad (1\beta)$$

where a and b are constants, is

$$m^2 + am + b = 0.$$

If the auxiliary equation has distinct roots m_1 and m_2, (1) has the solution

$$y = Ae^{m_1 x} + Be^{m_2 x}, \qquad\Bigg|\qquad u_n = Am_1^n + Bm_2^n,$$

where A and B are constants.

If the auxiliary equation has only one root m_1, (1) has the solution

$$y = (A + Bx)e^{m_1 x}. \qquad\Bigg|\qquad u_n = (A + Bn)m_1^n.$$

The general solution of

$$\frac{d^2y}{dx^2} + a\frac{dy}{dx} + by = \mathrm{f}(x) \qquad (2\alpha) \qquad\Bigg|\qquad u_{n+2} + au_{n+1} + bu_n = \mathrm{f}(n) \qquad (2\beta)$$

is the sum of any particular solution and a **complementary function**, which is the solution of (1).

For equation (2α) and continuous functions f:

If the **initial values** of both y and dy/dx are given for some x_0, there is certain to be a unique solution in some domain including x_0.

If the **boundary values** of either y or dy/dx are given at two values of x, there may be no solution, or one solution, or an infinity of solutions.

Errors

If x is an approximation to X then the **error** δ is defined by $X = x + \delta$. The **absolute error** is defined as $|\delta| = |X - x|$, and the **relative error** as $|\delta/X|$ if $X \neq 0$.

If x and y are approximations to X and Y with errors lying between $\pm\delta$ and $\pm\epsilon$ respectively, then

(i) the **maximum absolute error** in $x + y$ as an approximation to $X + Y$ is the sum $|\delta| + |\epsilon|$ of the absolute errors in x and y;

(ii) the **maximum relative error** in xy as an approximation to XY is (approximately) equal to the sum $|\delta/X| + |\epsilon/Y|$ of the relative errors in x and y, assuming that these are small.

Approximations to derivatives: If the derivatives exist, then for small h

$$f'(x) \approx \frac{f(x+h) - f(x-h)}{2h}$$

$$f''(x) \approx \frac{f(x+h) - 2f(x) + f(x-h)}{h^2}.$$

The errors are approximately $-h^2 f'''(x)/6$ and $-h^2 f^{(iv)}(x)/12$ provided that (respectively) f''' and $f^{(iv)}$ are continuous.

Approximations to definite integrals

(In these formulae, $x_i = x_0 + ih$ and $y_i = \mathrm{f}(x_i)$; $a = x_0$ and $b = x_n$.)

Trapezium rule: $$\int_{x_0}^{x_n} \mathrm{f}(x)\,dx \approx \tfrac{1}{2}h\{(y_0 + y_n) + 2(y_1 + y_2 + \ldots + y_{n-1})\}.$$

If f'' is continuous, the error is $-(b-a)h^2\,\mathrm{f}''(\theta)/12$, where θ is a number between a and b.

Simpson's rule, in which n must be *even*, giving an *odd* number of ordinates:

$$\int_{x_0}^{x_n} \mathrm{f}(x)\,dx \approx \tfrac{1}{3}h\{(y_0 + y_n) + 4(y_1 + y_3 + \ldots + y_{n-1}) + 2(y_2 + y_4 + \ldots + y_{n-2})\}.$$

If $\mathrm{f}^{(\mathrm{iv})}$ is continuous, the error is $-(b-a)h^4\,\mathrm{f}^{(\mathrm{iv})}(\phi)/180$, where ϕ is a number between a and b.

Approximate solution of differential equations

The **Euler** (or **simple step-by-step**) method for solving the differential equation $dy/dx = \mathrm{f}(x, y)$ with step length h uses

$$x_{\text{new}} = x_{\text{old}} + h, \quad y_{\text{new}} \approx y_{\text{old}} + hf(x_{\text{old}}, y_{\text{old}}).$$

The **modified Euler** (or **Heun**, or **trapezium**) **method** uses

$$x_{\text{new}} = x_{\text{old}} + h, \quad y_{\text{inter}} = y_{\text{old}} + hf(x_{\text{old}}, y_{\text{old}})$$

to give

$$y_{\text{new}} \approx y_{\text{old}} + \tfrac{1}{2}h\left\{\mathrm{f}(x_{\text{old}}, y_{\text{old}}) + \mathrm{f}(x_{\text{new}}, y_{\text{inter}})\right\}.$$

The **second-order linear equation**

$$\frac{d^2y}{dx^2} + \frac{a\,dy}{dx} + by = \mathrm{f}(x) \quad \text{is discretized as}$$

$$\frac{y_{i+1} - 2y_i + y_{i-1}}{h^2} + \frac{a(y_{i+1} - y_{i-1})}{2h} + by_i = \mathrm{f}(x_i)$$

where $x_i = x_0 + ih$ and y_i denotes the value of y when $x = x_i$.

Iterative processes

A convergent interactive process is said to have **first order convergence** when successive errors e_n *and* e_{n+1} satisfy

$$|e_{n+1}/e_n| \to K \quad \text{as } n \to \infty, \text{ with } 0 < K < 1.$$

Aitken's δ^2 acceleration process uses three iterates x_n, x_{n+1}, x_{n+2} in a first-order process to give a closer approximation to the limit of the process as

$$x_n - \frac{(\Delta x_n)^2}{\Delta^2 x_n},$$

where $\Delta x_n = x_{n+1} - x_n$ and $\Delta^2 x_n = x_{n+2} - 2x_{n+1} + x_n$.

Newton–Raphson method: If p_n is an approximation to a root of $f(x) = 0$, then

$$p_{n+1} = p_n - \frac{f(p_n)}{f'(p_n)}$$

is generally a better one. The error is approximately

$$-\frac{\{f(p_n)\}^2 f''(p_n)}{2\{f'(p_n)\}^3}$$

Solution of a set of linear algebraic equations

In **Jacobi iteration** the equations are arranged as

$$\mathbf{x} = \mathbf{A}\mathbf{x} + \mathbf{k},$$

where $\mathbf{A}$ is a matrix with small entries. The iteration process is

$$\mathbf{x}_{n+1} = \mathbf{A}\mathbf{x}_n + \mathbf{k}.$$

Jacobi iteration certainly converges

(i) if all the row sums of moduli of elements of $\mathbf{A}$ are less than 1, *or*

(ii) if all the column sums of the moduli are less than 1, *or*

(iii) if all the eigenvalues of $\mathbf{A}$ are less than 1 in modulus.

The iteration *may* also converge when either or both of (i) and (ii) are not satisfied.

In **Gauss–Seidel iteration** (successive displacements) the equations are arranged as

$$\mathbf{x} = \mathbf{L}\mathbf{x} + \mathbf{U}\mathbf{x} + \mathbf{k},$$

where $\mathbf{L}$ is a lower triangular matrix and $\mathbf{U}$ is an upper triangular matrix, both with small entries. The iteration process is

$$(\mathbf{I} - \mathbf{L})\mathbf{x}_{n+1} = \mathbf{U}\mathbf{x}_n + \mathbf{k}.$$

Gauss–Seidel iteration certainly converges under conditions (i) or (ii) for Jacobi iteration, with $\mathbf{A} = \mathbf{L} + \mathbf{U}$; it also converges

(iv) if all the eigenvalues of $(\mathbf{I} - \mathbf{L})^{-1}\mathbf{U}$ are less than 1 in modulus.

CONICS

Parabola

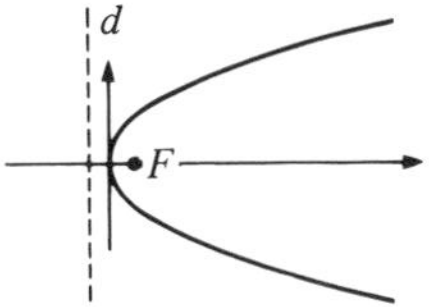

Ellipse

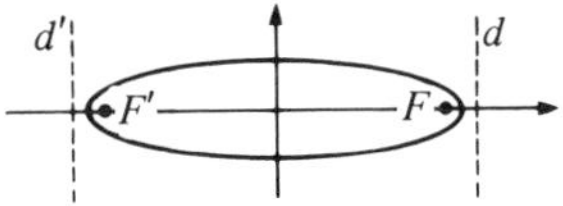

Hyperbola

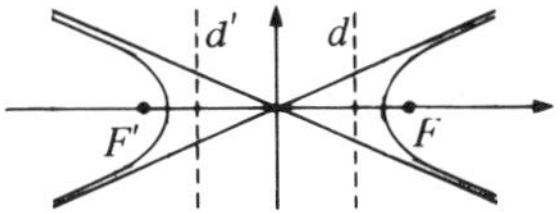

Rectangular hyperbola

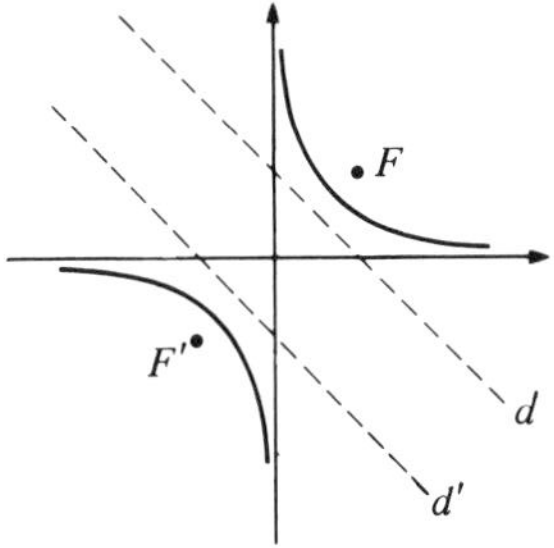

Name of curve	Standard form of equation	Standard parametric forms	Eccentricity e	Foci F and F'	Directrices d and d'	Asymptotes
Parabola	$y^2 = 4ax$	$(ap^2, 2ap)$	1	$(a, 0)$	$x = -a$	None
Ellipse	$\frac{x^2}{a^2} + \frac{y^2}{b^2} = 1$	$(a \cos\theta, b \sin\theta)$	$\frac{\sqrt{(a^2 - b^2)}}{a} < 1$	$(\pm ae, 0)$	$x = \pm\frac{a}{e}$	None
Circle	$x^2 + y^2 = a^2$	$(a \cos\theta, a \sin\theta)$	0	$(0, 0)$	None	None
Hyperbola	$\frac{x^2}{a^2} - \frac{y^2}{b^2} = 1$	$(a \sec\phi, b \tan\phi)$ or $(\pm a \cosh u, b \sinh u)$	$\frac{\sqrt{(a^2 + b^2)}}{a} > 1$	$(\pm ae, 0)$	$x = \pm\frac{a}{e}$	$\frac{x}{a} \pm \frac{y}{b} = 0$
Rectangular hyperbola	$xy = c^2$	$(cp, c/p)$	$\sqrt{2}$	$(\pm c\sqrt{2}, \pm c\sqrt{2})$	$x + y = \pm c\sqrt{2}$	$x = 0, y = 0$

The general second degree equation $ax^2 + 2hxy + by^2 + 2gx + 2fy + c = 0$ can be written in the matrix form $\mathbf{x}^{\mathrm{T}}\mathbf{M}\mathbf{x} = 0$, where

$$\mathbf{M} = \begin{bmatrix} a & h & g \\ h & b & f \\ g & f & c \end{bmatrix} \quad \text{and} \quad \mathbf{x} = \begin{bmatrix} x \\ y \\ 1 \end{bmatrix}.$$

Conditions for special conics (a, h, b not all zero):

Parabola	$ab - h^2 = 0$.	Circle	$a = b$ and $h = 0$.
Ellipse	$ab - h^2 > 0$.	Rectangular hyperbola	$a + b = 0$.
Hyperbola	$ab - h^2 < 0$.	Line-pair	$\det \mathbf{M} = 0$.

Polar equation

If the origin is taken at a focus of the conic, and the line $\theta = 0$ as the ray from that focus drawn towards the corresponding directrix, then the equation of the conic has the form

$$\frac{l}{r} = 1 + e\cos\theta,$$

where e is the eccentricity and l the length of the semi-latus rectum.

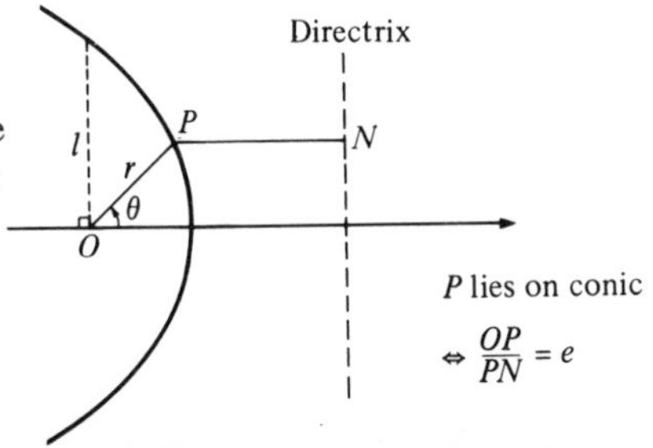

MECHANICS

Velocity and acceleration in two dimensions

($\mathbf{i}$, $\mathbf{j}$, $\hat{\mathbf{r}}$, $\hat{\mathbf{u}}$, $\hat{\mathbf{t}}$, $\hat{\mathbf{n}}$ are unit vectors. See also figure on p. 20.)

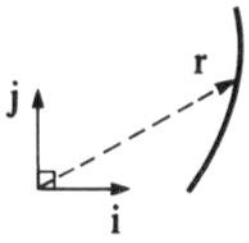

$\mathbf{r} = x\mathbf{i} + y\mathbf{j}$

$\mathbf{v} = \dot{x}\mathbf{i} + \dot{y}\mathbf{j}$

$\mathbf{a} = \ddot{x}\mathbf{i} + \ddot{y}\mathbf{j}$

Cartesian

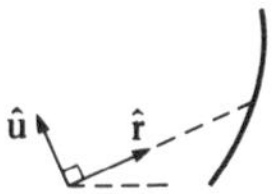

$\mathbf{r} = r\hat{\mathbf{r}}$

$\mathbf{v} = \dot{r}\hat{\mathbf{r}} + r\dot{\theta}\hat{\mathbf{u}}$

$\mathbf{a} = (\ddot{r} - r\dot{\theta}^2)\hat{\mathbf{r}} + (r\ddot{\theta} + 2\dot{r}\dot{\theta})\hat{\mathbf{u}}$

Polar (radial and transverse)

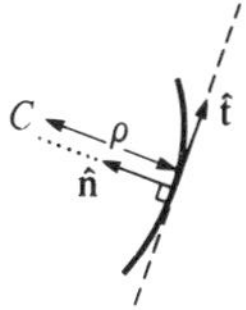

$\mathbf{v} = v\hat{\mathbf{t}}$

$\mathbf{a} = \dot{v}\hat{\mathbf{t}} + (v^2/\rho)\,\hat{\mathbf{n}}$

Intrinsic (tangential and normal)

Notes: (i) The transverse component of acceleration in polar form can be written as $\dfrac{1}{r}\dfrac{d}{dt}(r^2\dot{\theta})$.

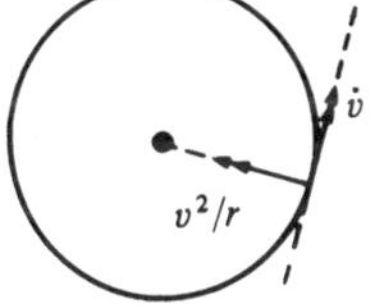

(ii) For motion in a circle (centre the origin), the components of acceleration in polar form are $\quad -r\dot{\theta}^2 = -v^2/r$ and $r\ddot{\theta} = \dot{v}$.

(iii) For motion in a line, $\quad v = \dot{x}, \quad a = \ddot{x} = v\dfrac{dv}{dx}$.

Motion with constant acceleration a

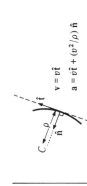

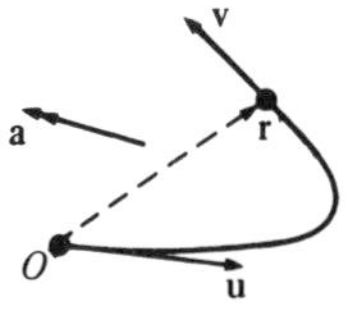

$$\mathbf{v} = \mathbf{u} + t\mathbf{a}; \quad v^2 = u^2 + 2\mathbf{a}\,.\,\mathbf{r}; \quad \mathbf{r} = t\mathbf{u} + \tfrac{1}{2}t^2\mathbf{a}; \quad \mathbf{r} = \tfrac{1}{2}t(\mathbf{u} + \mathbf{v});$$

where $\mathbf{u}$ is the value of $\mathbf{v}$ when $t = 0$, and the position at $t = 0$ is taken as origin.

Projectile (moving under gravity without resistance) from O with initial speed u at an angle θ to the horizontal.

Range on a horizontal plane $= \dfrac{u^2}{g} \sin 2\theta$.   Time of flight $= \dfrac{2u}{g} \sin \theta$.

Equation of trajectory: $y = x \tan \theta - \dfrac{gx^2}{2u^2} \sec^2 \theta$.

Newton's law of motion: $\mathbf{F} = m\mathbf{a}$ or $\dfrac{d}{dt}(m\mathbf{v})$ or $m\ddot{\mathbf{r}}$.

Impulse of a force, $\int \mathbf{F}\, dt$, is equal to the increase in momentum, $m\mathbf{v} - m\mathbf{u}$.

Newton's experimental law: At an impact, relative speed of separation $= e \times$ relative speed of approach, along the common normal. The constant e is called the **coefficient of restitution.**

Work done by a force, $\int \mathbf{F} \cdot \mathbf{v}\, dt$, is equal to the increase in kinetic energy, $\frac{1}{2}mv^2 - \frac{1}{2}mu^2$.
For a constant force, work done $= \mathbf{F} \cdot \mathbf{d}$, where $\mathbf{d}$ is the vector displacement.
For a force in the direction of motion along a straight line, work done $= \int_{x_1}^{x_2} F\, dx$.

Moment of a force $\mathbf{F}$, acting at a point with position vector $\mathbf{r}$, about O, is $\mathbf{r} \times \mathbf{F}$.

Moment of momentum about O of a particle with position vector $\mathbf{r}$ is $\mathbf{r} \times (m\mathbf{v})$.
For a rigid body rotating about O with angular velocity $\boldsymbol{\omega}$, the velocity of any point is $\boldsymbol{\omega} \times \mathbf{r}$.

Orbits (central force): $\mathbf{r} \times (m\mathbf{v}) = \mathbf{H}$, a constant vector, so that $2\dot{A} = r^2\dot{\theta} = pv = h$ (see figure on p. 20).
For an inverse square law of force μ/r^2, orbit is a conic with $l = h^2/\mu$ (see figure on p. 28)

PLANE AND SOLID FIGURES

(Mass M, of uniform density. G denotes centre of mass. I denotes moment of inertia about the axis indicated.)

Triangular lamina

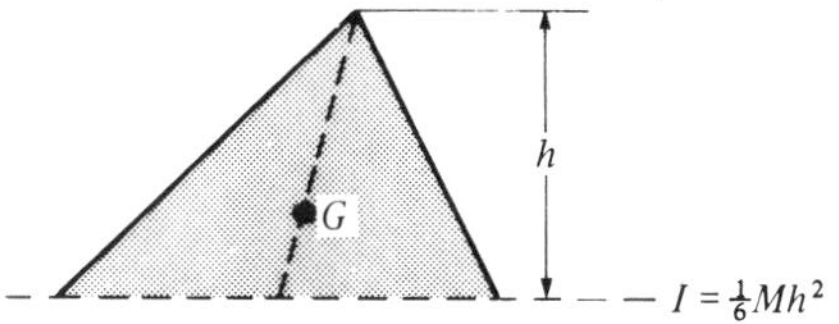

G is $\frac{1}{3}$ distance up the median

Rectangular lamina

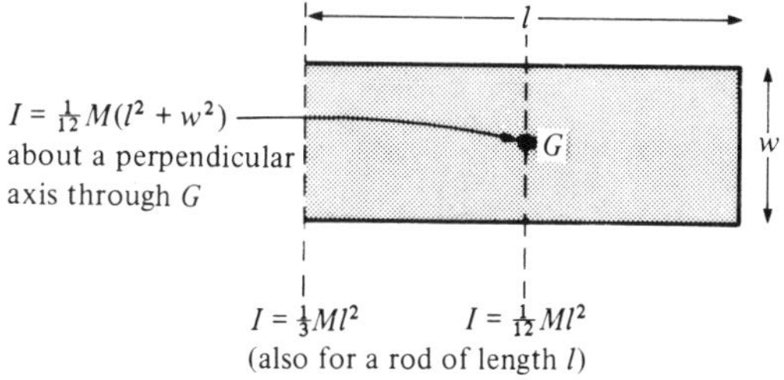

Circle

Hoop: Disc:

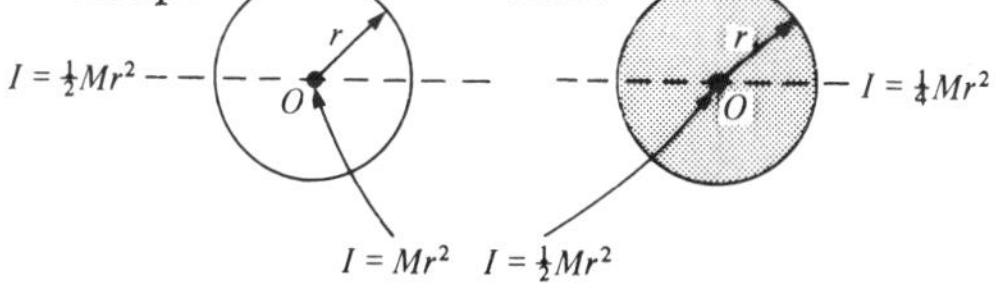

about a perpendicular axis through O

Arc:

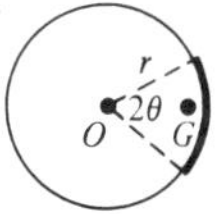

$$OG = r\frac{\sin\theta}{\theta}$$

Sector:

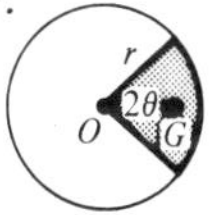

$$OG = \frac{2}{3}r\frac{\sin\theta}{\theta}$$

Sphere

Shell:

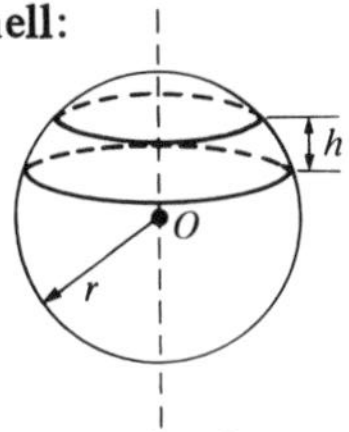

$I = \frac{2}{3}Mr^2$

Surface area = $4\pi r^2$

Surface area of zone between planes = $2\pi rh$

Solid:

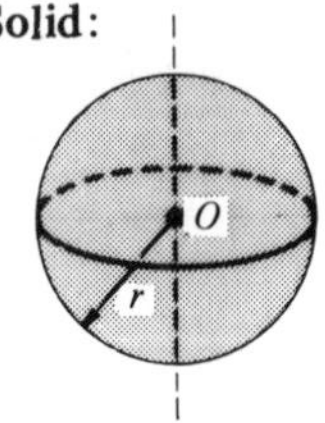

$I = \frac{2}{5}Mr^2$

Volume = $\frac{4}{3}\pi r^3$

For a hemispherical shell, $OG = \frac{1}{2}r$

For a solid hemisphere, $OG = \frac{3}{8}r$

Cylinder

Shell (curved surface only):

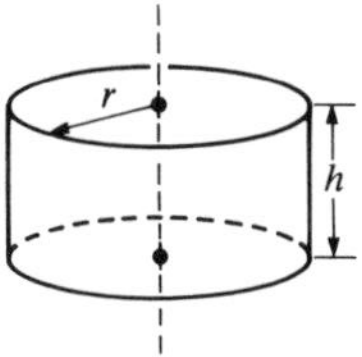

$I = Mr^2$

Solid:

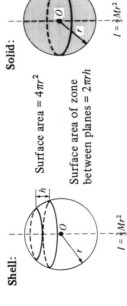

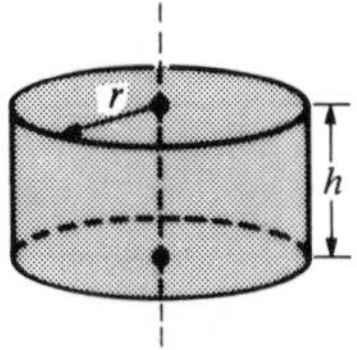

$I = \frac{1}{2}Mr^2$

Surface area = base perimeter × height (for any prism)
= $2\pi rh$

Volume = base area × height (for any prism)

= $\pi r^2 h$

Solid pyramid, including cone

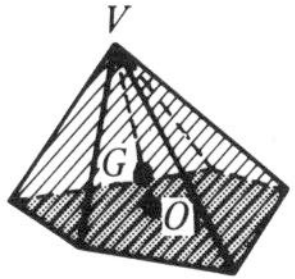

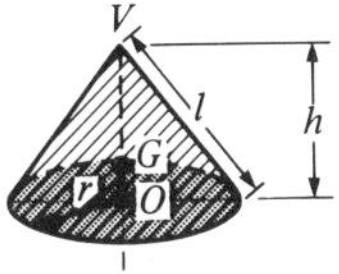

Surface area of cone $= \pi rl$.

Volume $= \frac{1}{3}$ base area × height

$= \frac{1}{3}\pi r^2 h$ for the cone.

G is $\frac{1}{4}$ distance up OV, where O is the centroid of the base.

Parallel axes rule: For any figure, $I_A = I_G + Md^2$, where d is the distance between the axes.

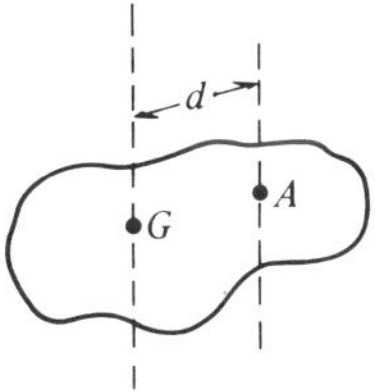

Perpendicular axes rule: For a *lamina*, $I_z = I_x + I_y$, where the x- and y-axes lie in the lamina.

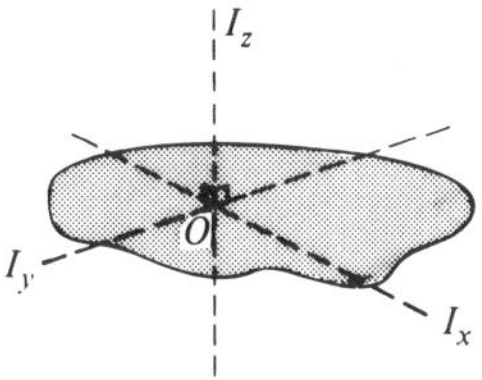

The **radius of gyration** is the length k such that $I = Mk^2$.

ELECTRICITY

Resistance: When a potential difference of V volts is applied across a resistor of resistance R ohms, the current flowing is I amperes, where

$$V = IR \text{ (Ohm's law)},$$

and the power consumed is P watts, where

$$P = VI = I^2R = V^2/R.$$

Capacitance: When a capacitor of capacitance C farads is charged to a potential difference of V volts, the charge on its positive plates is q coulombs, where

$$q = CV.$$

The energy stored in the capacitor in joules is

$$\tfrac{1}{2}qV = \tfrac{1}{2}CV^2 = \tfrac{1}{2}q^2/C.$$

Inductance: When a variable current i amperes flows through an inductor of inductance L henries, the induced electro-motive force e_L volts (which is negative if the current is increasing) is given by

$$e_L = -L\frac{di}{dt}.$$

Kirchhoff's first law: No current is lost at junctions.

Kirchhoff's second law: The algebraic sum of the potential differences round a closed circuit (making allowance for the battery voltage in the circuit) is zero.

The LCR circuit

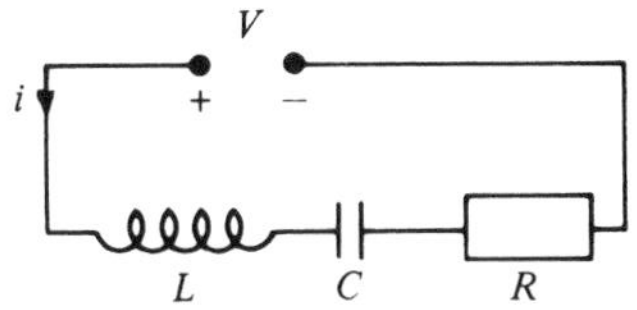

The current i and the charge q on the capacitor satisfy the differential equation

$$L\frac{di}{dt} + \frac{q}{C} + iR = V,$$

where $i = \dfrac{dq}{dt}$.

If the applied voltage is represented by the real part of $\mathbf{V} = V_0 \exp(j\omega t)$, then the current in the steady state is represented by the real part of $\mathbf{I} = \mathbf{V}/Z$, where

$$Z = R + j\omega L + \frac{1}{j\omega C} \quad \text{(the } \textbf{impedance}\text{)}.$$

The **frequency** f hertz is equal to $\omega/2\pi$.

PROBABILITY

$P(A \text{ and } B) + P(A \text{ and } {\sim}B) = P(A)$; $P(A \text{ or } B) = P(A) + P(B) - P(A \text{ and } B)$.

Conditional probability: $P(A|B) = P(A \text{ and } B)/P(B)$.

Bayes' theorem: $$P(A|B) = \frac{P(B|A) \times P(A)}{P(B|A) \times P(A) + P(B|{\sim}A) \times P({\sim}A)}.$$

Parameters

Mean $\mu = E(X) = \Sigma x_i p(x_i)$ or $\int x\phi(x)\,dx$ (evaluated over the possibility space).

Variance $\sigma^2 = V(X) = E((X-\mu)^2) = E(X^2) - \mu^2 = \Sigma x_i^2 p(x_i) - \mu^2$ or $\int x^2\phi(x)\,dx - \mu^2$.

Expectation

For a single random variable, $E(aX+b) = aE(X) + b$, $V(aX+b) = a^2V(X)$.

For two random variables, $E(X \pm Y) = E(X) \pm E(Y)$, $V(X \pm Y) = V(X) + V(Y) \pm 2\,\text{cov}(X, Y)$,

where the covariance $\text{cov}(X, Y) = E((X-\mu_X)(Y-\mu_Y)) = E(XY) - \mu_X\mu_Y$.

If X, Y are independent, $\text{cov}(X, Y) = 0$ so that $V(X \pm Y) = V(X) + V(Y)$.

Generators

If $G(t)$ is a **probability generator** for a random variable X, so that $G(t) = E(t^X) = \Sigma t^{x_i} p(x_i)$, then $\mu = G'(1)$; $\sigma^2 = G''(1) + \mu - \mu^2$.

The **moment generator** about the origin

Discrete

	Parameter	Probability p(i)	Probability generator	Mean	Variance	Meaning of p(i)
Binomial B(n, a)	P(success) = a P(failure) = b $[a + b = 1]$	$\frac{n!}{i!j!} a^i b^j$ $[i + j = n]$	$(b + at)^n$	na	nab	Probability of i successes in n independent trials
Geometric		ab^{i-1} $[i \geqslant 1]$	$at/(1 - bt)$	$1/a$	b/a^2	Probability that the first success occurs at the ith trial
Poisson	Mean λ in unit interval	$\frac{\lambda^i}{i!} e^{-\lambda}$ $[i \geqslant 0]$	$e^{\lambda(t-1)}$	λ	λ	Probability of i occurrences in unit interval

Continuous

	Probability density $\phi(x)$	Moment generator	Mean	Variance	Application and table
Negative exponential	$\lambda e^{-\lambda x}$ $[x \geqslant 0]$	$1/(1 - u/\lambda)$	$1/\lambda$	$1/\lambda^2$	–
Normal N(μ, σ^2)	$\frac{1}{\sigma\sqrt{(2\pi)}} e^{-(x-\mu)^2/2\sigma^2}$	$e^{\mu u + \sigma^2 u^2/2}$	μ	σ^2	pp. 41–43
Student's t (ν d.f.)	$C_\nu(\nu + t^2)^{-(\nu+1)/2}$	–	0	$\nu/(\nu - 2)$ $[\nu > 2]$	pp. 44–45
χ^2 (ν d.f.)	$B_\nu x^{(\nu/2)-1} e^{-x/2}$	$(1 - 2u)^{-\nu/2}$	ν	2ν	pp. 46–47

The constants B_ν, C_ν are chosen to make the total probability equal to 1.

Binomial coefficients $\binom{n}{i}$

n \ i	0	1	2	3	4	5	6	7	8	9	10
1	1	1									
2	1	2	1								
3	1	3	3	1							
4	1	4	6	4	1						
5	1	5	10	10	5	1					
6	1	6	15	20	15	6	1				
7	1	7	21	35	35	21	7	1			
8	1	8	28	56	70	56	28	8	1		
9	1	9	36	84	126	126	84	36	9	1	
10	1	10	45	120	210	252	210	120	45	10	1
11	1	11	55	165	330	462	462	330	165	55	11
12	1	12	66	220	495	792	924	792	495	220	66
13	1	13	78	286	715	1287	1716	1716	1287	715	286
14	1	14	91	364	1001	2002	3003	3432	3003	2002	1001
15	1	15	105	455	1365	3003	5005	6435	6435	5005	3003
16	1	16	120	560	1820	4368	8008	11440	12870	11440	8008
17	1	17	136	680	2380	6188	12376	19448	24310	24310	19448
18	1	18	153	816	3060	8568	18564	31824	43758	48620	43758
19	1	19	171	969	3876	11628	27132	50388	75582	92378	92378
20	1	20	190	1140	4845	15504	38760	77520	125970	167960	184756

89 90	26 36	22 74	71 13	74 05	58 67	79 59	34 69	67 51	58 57	76 58	17 38
86 38	25 76	20 69	35 84	53 73	47 38	46 54	91 63	33 65	25 02	32 03	66 23
98 10	31 80	82 41	41 82	54 76	90 22	95 78	25 58	06 68	19 49	08 95	74 83
94 18	87 43	71 84	45 45	96 43	59 63	23 13	54 79	61 67	36 37	33 26	87 75
33 69	26 21	93 49	56 64	25 68	49 58	90 47	33 17	19 56	33 36	11 72	19 09
85 71	59 36	22 42	88 11	63 09	63 24	95 76	07 89	89 07	73 09	74 88	23 55
32 25	01 53	36 19	10 42	49 50	98 75	38 88	65 44	00 45	88 37	41 62	84 72
17 85	78 43	44 60	69 05	86 59	66 98	92 56	79 88	70 45	05 62	17 74	81 88
04 50	22 00	74 57	49 82	75 34	25 90	05 50	24 63	30 64	31 84	66 19	83 47
79 91	04 95	34 45	08 62	83 99	81 26	89 40	61 49	94 30	94 66	08 26	10 42
48 01	83 62	70 23	81 29	23 84	38 91	91 50	19 93	25 54	61 74	26 05	34 65
95 14	63 02	09 68	89 66	32 52	16 05	39 39	02 71	55 99	16 45	98 67	01 58
58 51	58 85	13 72	52 57	84 58	66 68	32 58	66 07	78 74	93 42	81 93	73 32
88 50	46 86	70 24	86 62	38 78	33 76	68 20	67 61	29 72	52 17	44 56	96 53
16 54	05 64	73 80	20 83	44 09	66 51	28 72	97 48	68 60	20 96	55 47	55 73
20 73	33 39	25 44	19 13	68 71	26 81	25 14	30 75	74 61	56 70	93 47	12 50
47 38	74 44	92 47	37 84	03 89	26 23	52 41	06 59	38 43	03 46	88 95	91 96
58 17	60 57	02 99	45 72	45 42	61 47	15 18	73 12	98 26	83 31	83 99	24 07
26 81	50 42	24 97	87 14	89 71	83 17	14 93	46 12	16 74	95 10	99 87	21 05
95 64	20 88	42 63	17 25	80 41	33 22	25 83	65 08	33 05	89 61	29 86	12 19
29 80	09 62	33 60	64 44	31 22	31 70	18 11	07 85	70 74	91 17	91 45	76 77
70 46	91 35	07 77	27 84	40 20	77 25	44 00	03 23	45 60	02 22	61 67	08 49
96 67	06 01	60 64	69 46	17 69	27 55	98 32	05 66	88 46	68 25	87 25	14 16
12 25	05 68	84 84	62 91	23 97	99 19	93 94	66 51	22 45	41 59	66 80	62 63
18 65	57 35	74 25	81 35	62 62	01 43	74 05	88 51	53 69	88 78	15 71	96 11

This table produces sequences of digits 0 to 9 in an order which may be used to simulate the drawing of digits from a population in which each has a probability of $\frac{1}{10}$.

STATISTICS

Statistical measures

If n is the sample size and $f(x_i)$ the frequency of occurrence of the value x_i in the sample (so that $n = \Sigma f(x_i)$), then:

Sample mean m (or $\bar{x}$) $= \frac{1}{n} \sum_i x_i f(x_i)$.

Sample variance v (or S^2) $= \frac{1}{n} \sum_i (x_i - m)^2 f(x_i) = \frac{1}{n} \sum_i x_i^2 f(x_i) - m^2$.

Sample standard deviation S is the square root of the variance.

(**Note**: Some statisticians define the sample variance as $nv/(n-1)$, denoted by s^2. Other results involving the statistic s will, of course, take different forms from those involving S as here defined. A calculator with a built-in program may use either convention.)

Sample covariance $C_{x,y} = \frac{1}{n} \sum_i \sum_j (x_i - \bar{x})(y_j - \bar{y}) f(x_i, y_j) = \frac{1}{n} \sum_i \sum_j x_i y_j f(x_i, y_j) - \bar{x}\bar{y}$.

Least squares regression line of y on x passes through $(\bar{x}, \bar{y})$ and has gradient $C_{x,y}/S_x^2$.

Product-moment correlation coefficient $r = C_{x,y}/S_x S_y$.

Rank correlation coefficients for two separate rankings of n individuals:

Spearman's $r = 1 - \{6 \Sigma (\text{difference in ranks})^2 / n(n^2 - 1)\}$.

Estimation of population parameters

If the parent population has mean μ and standard deviation σ, the sample means constitute a population with mean μ and standard deviation $\sigma/\sqrt{n}$ of approximately Normal form (for large n); and the sample variances constitute a population with mean $\{(n-1)/n\}\sigma^2$.

Unbiased estimator of mean, $\hat{\mu} = m$.

Unbiased estimator of variance, $\widehat{\sigma^2} = \{n/(n-1)\}S^2 = s^2$ (see the note on p. 40)

Statistical applications (1) Normal probability

The following statistics have, for large samples, approximate Normal probability density N(0, 1).

(i) Interval estimate of population mean: $\dfrac{m-\mu}{S/\sqrt{n}}$.

(ii) Significance of difference of sample means: $\dfrac{m_1 - m_2}{\sqrt{\left(\dfrac{S_1^2}{n_1} + \dfrac{S_2^2}{n_2}\right)}}$.

(iii) Significance of difference of sample proportions p_1, p_2:

$$\frac{(p_1 - p_2)\sqrt{\{n_1 n_2 (n_1 + n_2)\}}}{\sqrt{\{(n_1 p_1 + n_2 p_2)(n_1 q_1 + n_2 q_2)\}}} \quad \text{(where } q = 1 - p\text{)}.$$

(iv) If r is the product-moment correlation coefficient: $z\sqrt{(n-3)}$, where $z = \frac{1}{2}\ln\dfrac{1+r}{1-r}$.

(v) If τ is the Kendall's rank correlation coefficient: $\tau\sqrt{\dfrac{9n(n-1)}{2(2n+5)}}$.

Normal probability N(0, 1)

Table of cumulative probability $\Phi(x)$

x	0	1	2	3	4	5	6	7	8	9
0.0	.500	.504	.508	.512	.516	.520	.524	.528	.532	.536
0.1	.540	.544	.548	.552	.556	.560	.564	.567	.571	.575
0.2	.579	.583	.587	.591	.595	.599	.603	.606	.610	.614
0.3	.618	.622	.626	.629	.633	.637	.641	.644	.648	.652
0.4	.655	.659	.663	.666	.670	.674	.677	.681	.684	.688
0.5	.691	.695	.698	.702	.705	.709	.712	.716	.719	.722
0.6	.726	.729	.732	.736	.739	.742	.745	.749	.752	.755
0.7	.758	.761	.764	.767	.770	.773	.776	.779	.782	.785
0.8	.788	.791	.794	.797	.800	.802	.805	.808	.811	.813
0.9	.816	.819	.821	.824	.826	.829	.831	.834	.836	.839
1.0	.841	.844	.846	.848	.851	.853	.855	.858	.860	.862
1.1	.864	.867	.869	.871	.873	.875	.877	.879	.881	.883
1.2	.885	.887	.889	.891	.893	.894	.896	.898	.900	.901
1.3	.903	.905	.907	.908	.910	.911	.913	.915	.916	.918
1.4	.919	.921	.922	.924	.925	.926	.928	.929	.931	.932
1.5	.933	.934	.936	.937	.938	.939	.941	.942	.943	.944
1.6	.945	.946	.947	.948	.949	.951	.952	.953	.954	.954
1.7	.955	.956	.957	.958	.959	.960	.961	.962	.962	.963
1.8	.964	.965	.966	.966	.967	.968	.969	.969	.970	.971
1.9	.971	.972	.973	.973	.974	.974	.975	.976	.976	.977

2.0	.9772	.9778	.9783	.9788	.9793	.9798	.9803	.9808	.9812	.9817
2.1	.9821	.9826	.9830	.9834	.9838	.9842	.9846	.9850	.9854	.9857
2.2	.9861	.9864	.9868	.9871	.9875	.9878	.9881	.9884	.9887	.9890
2.3	.9893	.9896	.9898	.9901	.9904	.9906	.9909	.9911	.9913	.9916
2.4	.9918	.9920	.9922	.9925	.9927	.9929	.9931	.9932	.9934	.9936
2.5	.9938	.9940	.9941	.9943	.9945	.9946	.9948	.9949	.9951	.9952
2.6	.9953	.9955	.9956	.9957	.9959	.9960	.9961	.9962	.9963	.9964
2.7	.9965	.9966	.9967	.9968	.9969	.9970	.9971	.9972	.9973	.9974
2.8	.9974	.9975	.9976	.9977	.9977	.9978	.9979	.9979	.9980	.9981
2.9	.9981	.9982	.9982	.9983	.9984	.9984	.9985	.9985	.9986	.9986
3.0	.9987	.9987	.9987	.9988	.9988	.9989	.9989	.9989	.9990	.9990

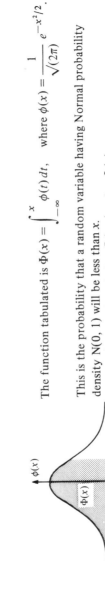

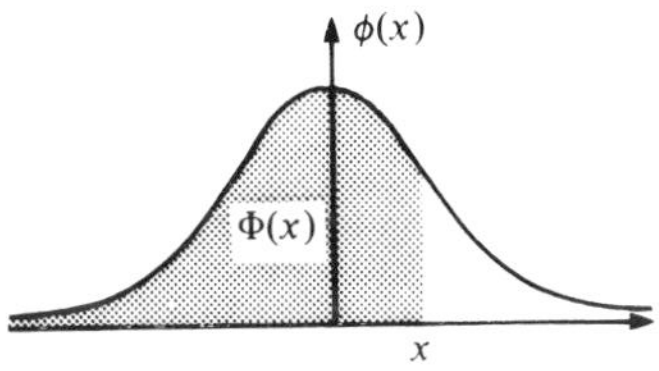

The function tabulated is $\Phi(x) = \int_{-\infty}^{x} \phi(t)\,dt$, where $\phi(x) = \frac{1}{\sqrt{(2\pi)}} e^{-x^2/2}$.

This is the probability that a random variable having Normal probability density N(0, 1) will be less than x.

If $x < 0$, use the relation $\Phi(-x) = 1 - \Phi(x)$.

Critical percentage points for Normal probability

$\Phi(x)$	95%	97.5%	99%	99.5%	99.9%	99.95%
$1 - \Phi(x)$ (one-tail tests)	5%	2.5%	1%	0.5%	0.1%	0.05%
$2(1 - \Phi(x))$ (two-tail tests)	10%	5%	2%	1%	0.2%	0.1%
x	1.6449	1.9600	2.3263	2.5758	3.0902	3.2905

t-probability

P	20	10	5	2	1	0.2	0.1
$\nu =$ 1	3.08	6.31	12.7	31.8	63.7	318	637
2	1.89	2.92	4.30	6.96	9.93	22.3	31.6
3	1.64	2.35	3.18	4.54	5.84	10.2	12.9
4	1.53	2.13	2.78	3.75	4.60	7.17	8.61
5	1.48	2.02	2.57	3.36	4.03	5.89	6.87
6	1.44	1.94	2.45	3.14	3.71	5.21	5.96
7	1.42	1.89	2.36	3.00	3.50	4.79	5.41
8	1.40	1.86	2.31	2.90	3.36	4.50	5.04
9	1.38	1.83	2.26	2.82	3.25	4.30	4.78
10	1.37	1.81	2.23	2.76	3.17	4.14	4.59
11	1.36	1.80	2.20	2.72	3.11	4.02	4.44
12	1.36	1.78	2.18	2.68	3.05	3.93	4.32
13	1.35	1.77	2.16	2.65	3.01	3.85	4.22
14	1.35	1.76	2.14	2.62	2.98	3.79	4.14
15	1.34	1.75	2.13	2.60	2.95	3.73	4.07
20	1.33	1.72	2.09	2.53	2.85	3.55	3.85
30	1.31	1.70	2.04	2.46	2.75	3.39	3.65
40	1.30	1.68	2.02	2.42	2.70	3.31	3.55
50	1.30	1.68	2.01	2.40	2.68	3.26	3.50
60	1.30	1.67	2.00	2.39	2.66	3.23	3.46
∞	1.28	1.64	1.96	2.33	2.58	3.09	3.29

The values for $\nu = \infty$ are those from a Normal probability function, which is the limiting form for large ν.

If X is a random variable with probability density function that of t with ν degrees of freedom, then $P/100$ is the probability that $|X| \geqslant t_P$. It is tabulated for two-tail tests. For one-tail tests, the probability that $X \geqslant t_P$ is half that given at the head of the table.

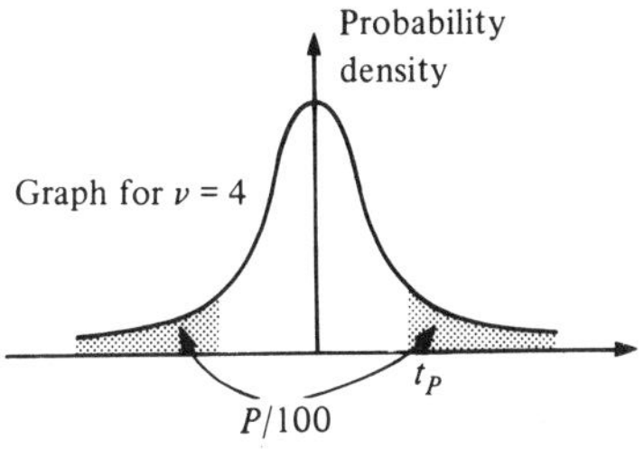

Statistical applications (2) t-probability

For samples *drawn from a Normal population*:

(vi) Interval estimate of population mean: $\dfrac{m-\mu}{S/\sqrt{\nu}}$, where $\nu = n-1$,

has t-probability density with ν degrees of freedom.

(vii) Significance of difference of sample means:

$$\frac{(m_1 - m_2)\sqrt{\nu}}{\sqrt{\left(\dfrac{1}{n_1} + \dfrac{1}{n_2}\right)} \cdot \sqrt{(n_1 S_1^2 + n_2 S_2^2)}}, \quad \text{where } \nu = n_1 + n_2 - 2,$$

has t-probability density with ν degrees of freedom.

(viii) Significance of product-moment correlation coefficient:

$$\frac{r\sqrt{\nu}}{\sqrt{(1-r^2)}}, \quad \text{where } \nu = n-2,$$

has t-probability density with ν degrees of freedom.

χ^2-probability

P	99	97.5	95	10	5	2.5	1	0.1
$\nu =$ 1	0.000157	0.000982	0.00393	2.71	3.84	5.02	6.63	10.83
2	0.0201	0.0506	0.103	4.61	5.99	7.38	9.21	13.82
3	0.115	0.216	0.352	6.25	7.81	9.35	11.34	16.27
4	0.297	0.484	0.711	7.78	9.49	11.14	13.28	18.47
5	0.554	0.831	1.15	9.24	11.07	12.83	15.09	20.52
6	0.872	1.24	1.64	10.64	12.59	14.45	16.81	22.46
7	1.24	1.69	2.17	12.02	14.07	16.01	18.48	24.32
8	1.65	2.18	2.73	13.36	15.51	17.53	20.09	26.12
9	2.09	2.70	3.33	14.68	16.92	19.02	21.67	27.88
10	2.56	3.25	3.94	15.99	18.31	20.48	23.21	29.59
11	3.05	3.82	4.57	17.28	19.68	21.92	24.72	31.26
12	3.57	4.40	5.23	18.55	21.03	23.34	26.22	32.91
13	4.11	5.01	5.89	19.81	22.36	24.74	27.69	34.53
14	4.66	5.63	6.57	21.06	23.68	26.12	29.14	36.12
15	5.23	6.26	7.26	22.31	25.00	27.45	30.58	37.70
20	8.26	9.59	10.85	28.41	31.41	34.17	37.57	45.31
30	14.95	16.79	18.49	40.26	43.77	46.98	50.89	59.70
40	22.16	24.43	26.51	51.81	55.76	59.34	63.69	73.40
50	29.71	32.36	34.76	63.17	67.50	71.42	76.15	86.66
60	37.48	40.48	43.19	74.40	79.08	83.30	88.38	99.61

For large values of ν linear interpolation or extrapolation is adequate.

If X is a random variable with probability density function that of χ^2 with ν degrees of freedom, then $P/100$ is the probability that $X \geqslant \chi_P^2$.

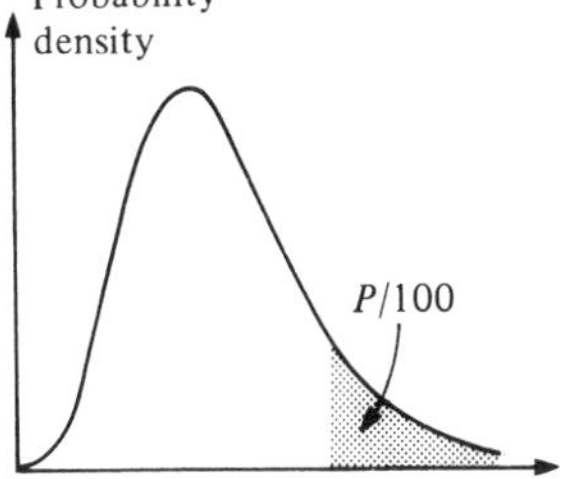

Statistical applications (3) χ^2-probability

(ix) Goodness of fit: If $f_e(X_i)$ denotes the expected frequency of an event $X_i (i = 1, 2, 3, \ldots)$ and $f_0(X_i)$ the observed frequency, then the discrepancy

$$\sum \frac{\{f_o(X_i) - f_e(X_i)\}^2}{f_e(X_i)} = \sum \frac{\{f_o(X_i)\}^2}{f_e(X_i)} - N \quad \text{(where } N \text{ is the total frequency)}$$

has approximately χ^2-probability density, provided that none of the $f_e(X_i)$ is very small. The number of degrees of freedom is the number of categories less 1 for each constraint (e.g. total, mean); when testing for independence in an $m \times n$ contingency table, $\nu = (m-1)(n-1)$.

(x) Interval estimate of population variance: If S^2 is the variance of a random sample drawn from a Normal population, nS^2/σ^2 has χ^2-probability density with $\nu = n - 1$.

INDEX